DANGER ZONE

Enemy Fire

by ANTHONY MASTERS
Illustrated by Tim Sell

This edition 2010

Franklin Watts
338 Euston Road
London
NW1 3BH

Franklin Watts Australia
Level 17/207 Kent Street
Sydney NSW 2000

Cover design: Peter Scoulding

Cover image: Andrew Howe/iStockphoto

A CIP catalogue record for
this book is available from
the British Library.

ISBN: 978 0 7496 9493 7

Dewey Classification: 956.7'0442'0922

10 9 8 7 6 5 4 3 2 1

Printed in Great Britain

Franklin Watts is a division of Hachette Children's Books,
an Hachette UK company.

www.hachette.co.uk

Contents

DANGER ZONE
FACT FILE

LOCATION

Iraqi desert during the Gulf War

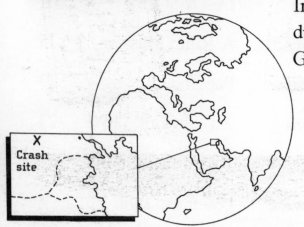

X
Crash site

DANGER

Discovery by Iraqi troops

PERSONNEL

John Peters and
John Nichol

John Peters
Pilot

John Nichol
Navigator

HAZARDS

! In enemy territory
! Loss of liquid
! Intense heat
! Injuries
! Survival equipment obvious to the enemy
! Plane wreckage obvious to the enemy
! Leaving tell-tale footprints in the sand
! Personal location beacons' transmissions
might be picked up by the enemy

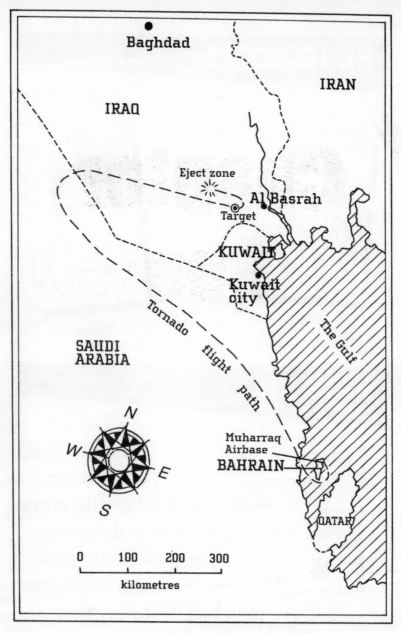

Map showing Tornado flight path and
ejection zone

6

Chapter One

Blown Sideways

January 17th, 1991

Peters turned the Tornado through sixty degrees. He and his navigator, Nichol, needed to make a fast escape.

The enemy SAM-16 missile, travelling at twice the speed of sound, was fired at the Tornado.

■ On impact

The missile's infra-red warhead locked on to the heat of the Tornado's engines. It pierced the heart of its right turbine.

The missile's titanium-laced explosive vaporized on impact and the thirty-ton Tornado was blown sideways.

Chapter Two

Desert Storm

The Tornado jet fighter was flying over
the Iraqi desert at 540 knots. The Gulf War
was raging. It had started after the Iraqi
president, Saddam Hussein, invaded his
neighbouring country, Kuwait.

The United Nations (UN) had passed a
Resolution insisting that Iraqi forces leave
Kuwait. Britain had joined the USA and
other UN countries to support this. The
war against Iraq was code-named
Operation Desert Storm.

▪ Friendly airspace

The Tornado's pilot was RAF Flight
Lieutenant John Peters and his navigator
was RAF Flight Lieutenant John Nichol.

They had just attacked an airfield in south-
western Iraq.

Now they were faced with a life-or-death
decision.

The Tornado was badly damaged. They
would have to eject. But the question
was when.

Both Peters and Nichol knew that they had
to make an attempt to fly on. They had to
reach friendly Saudi airspace. They didn't
want to eject and parachute down into
enemy territory.

■ Avoiding capture

In peacetime, the crew of a badly damaged aircraft would normally eject if one engine was on fire. But in wartime, it is considered essential to fly on to avoid capture.

Peters and Nichol desperately hoped the fire in the engine would burn itself out.

■ A problem

Each of the Tornado's engines sat in a shell made from titanium. This should have stopped the fire from spreading. Modern plane fuel doesn't catch fire easily.

There should have been no problem flying the plane on the one remaining engine.

But there was a problem.

Chapter
Three

A Radio Message

To their horror, Peters and Nichol soon discovered that the fire had spread. It had taken hold of the tail and right wing.

They knew they would have to face 'banging out' (ejecting from the aircraft) over enemy territory.

Peters wanted to give the order to eject at
once. Nichol made him wait until he had
worked out their exact location.

Nichol radioed their position back to their formation leader.

John Nichol hoped that once they had ejected on to the desert floor, a Black Hawk Special Forces helicopter would find them quickly.

■ Winched to safety?

Then, they would be winched up as soon as possible. Meanwhile, fighter cover would keep the Iraqis away.

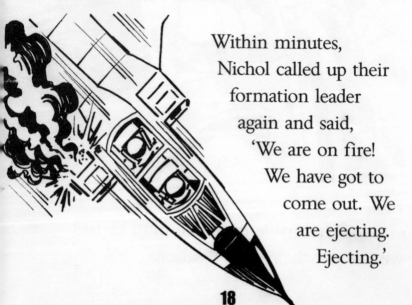

Within minutes, Nichol called up their formation leader again and said, 'We are on fire! We have got to come out. We are ejecting. Ejecting.'

Chapter
Four

Banging Out

Peters gave the official order to Nichol to eject. 'Prepare to eject. Prepare to eject. Three. Two. One. Eject! Eject!'

They both pulled hard at the handles between their legs. Then Nichol and Peters heard a faint mechanical thud. The restraining straps whipped around them.

Their arms and legs were pulled tightly against the frame of their seats. The ejection rockets fired.

Nichol and Peters were tossed high in the air at thirty times the force of gravity. The wind rush was deafening. There was a roaring sound from the seat rocket motors.

■ A feeling of falling

Peters later tried to sum up the feeling.

'Try putting your hand out of the car window at seventy miles per hour, then multiply that sensation by . . . six. There is a feeling of falling, endlessly falling, somersaulting end over end.'

■ A jarring crack

Finally, a small parachute was released to slow the fall. Then the main parachutes opened as the seats came upright.

Nichol and Peters felt a jarring crack as their parachute canopies opened.

There was a strong jerk as the parachutes took their weight.

Chapter
Five

An Obvious Target

Both pilot and navigator slowly drifted
down into enemy territory.

As he floated down, Nichol saw the
Tornado hit the desert floor. It burst into
a ball of flame. This was followed by a
column of dense black smoke.

Nichol reckoned that they could not have
advertised their arrival to the enemy any
better if they had tried!

■ Landing

Peters and Nichol both knew they had to concentrate on landing. This was made more difficult because they were carrying heavy packs.

They had heard about a pilot who had ejected without shedding his pack in time. He had broken both his legs when he landed.

■ Winded

They were both careful to pull their release straps before landing. Their packs hit the ground first.

Nichol was winded when he fell. Peters hurt his leg and cut the top of his left eye.

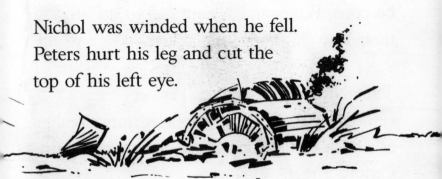

They laughed uncontrollably as they looked around them at the burning Tornado and their scattered survival equipment. What an obvious target they made!

▪ Camouflage!

Their parachutes were billowing on the desert floor. They also had the packs plus life-jackets, water-bags and helmets.

Worse still, to reach their personal location beacons, Peters and Nichol had to inflate their Day-glo orange life-jackets.

John Nichol later wrote: 'Perfect camouflage, of course: about as unnoticeable as a pack of baboons Christmas shopping on Oxford Street.'

Chapter
Six

Buried in the Sand

Nichol started transmitting on the beacons. He gave their bearings and said they were both safe.

He prayed that the signals would not be received by the enemy. He hoped the RAF rescue helicopter would come soon.

A nasty thought

To get at the rest of their survival box, they had to inflate their dinghies. These, along with the life-jackets, were provided in case they ditched over the sea.

This made them laugh helplessly again.

Peters and Nichol soon stopped laughing when a nasty thought came to them.

Sitting targets

The missile that had shot down the Tornado had come up from behind them. This meant that it must have been fired from the ground.

Iraqi troops were probably already searching for them. They were sitting targets.

Wading through treacle

They quickly hacked at their life-jackets with John Peters' Swiss Army penknife. Then they started to slash at the dinghies. When both were finally deflated, they buried them in the sand.

Putting on their haversacks, they checked their pistols. They began to stumble through the deep sand of the desert. It was like wading through treacle.

Dehydrated

The Sun was also very hot. Both Peters' and Nichol's flying suits made them sweat. They quickly became dehydrated - desperate for liquid.

Peters was limping badly.

Chapter Seven

Leaving a Trail

Nichol and Peters walked for an hour.
They left huge footprints in the sand.

John Nichol later wrote that the footprints
read, 'Enemy officers this way!' But what
else could they do?

The only solution might have been to go
down on their hands and knees. Even this
would still have left a trail.

■ Enemy hands

Nichol remembered he was carrying his route map. This must not be allowed to fall into the hands of the enemy.

Despite his dry throat, he tried to eat a section of the map. He buried the rest of it in the sand.

Then, they saw an armoured personnel carrier driving towards them.

Flattening themselves on the ground, they could also make out a red pick-up truck and a line of men.

■ Search party

The Iraqi search party was armed with powerful guns - AK-47s.

Nichol and Peters tried to dig themselves into the sand as bullets cracked over their heads. But they knew they didn't stand a chance.

They got to their feet, hands raised.

The firing began again.

■ Bewildered

Bewildered, Peters and Nichol threw themselves to the ground again. An Iraqi officer shouted in English: 'Stop. Give yourselves in.'

■ Surrender

Nichol realised that in the confusion the Iraqi officer had thought the two British airforce officers were firing back. Yet they had been raising their hands in surrender.

Shaking, they stood up for the second time. The bullets stopped.

■ Tied

The Iraqi patrol took Nichol's radio and
Peters' gun. They took the £1,000 survival
money in gold coins from Nichol, as well as
his flying watch.

They tied Peters' and Nichol's hands behind
their backs and forced them into the red
pick-up truck.

Three Bedouin trackers and a boy of about twelve arrived. The Bedouin make good trackers. The desert is their home so they know the landscape well.

■ From the skies

One of the Bedouin began to yell at Nichol and punched him in the face. The Iraqi officer stopped him being beaten to death. He wanted his prisoners alive.

The Bedouin boy was bouncing about. The Iraqi officer explained, 'He is very excited. You came from the skies.'

Chapter Eight

Daylight Raids

On January 17th, 1991, an international news service reported:

A British Tornado fighter-bomber has been lost during raids on Iraqi targets, according to military sources . . . it was understood to be the first loss out of seventy-five British warplanes in the region in Thursday's fighting.

The precise location of the incident and the fate of the two crew are unknown.

The aircraft was engaged in a second wave of daylight raids after the initial attacks under cover of darkness.

The Iraqis drove Peters and Nichol back to the area where they had parachuted down.

Despite the fact that they had walked for two or three hours, the truck only took three minutes to get back to the place where they had landed.

They had only covered 500 metres.

■ Gun in hand

As the pick-up truck drove on, the Bedouin boy sat in the back with a gun in his hand. He kept drawing his finger across his throat.

It was not a reassuring sight.

▪ Battered faces

RAF Flight Lieutenants John Peters and John Nichol were badly tortured by their Iraqi captors. But they were not killed.

Later, Iraqi television transmitted their battered faces across the world.

■ Terrible conditions

They were held for seven weeks in terrible conditions. Their Iraqi captors beat them to try to get military secrets out of them. But neither Peters nor Nichol gave way.

The two British airforce crew were released at the end of the Gulf War when Iraqi leader Saddam Hussein surrendered in March 1991.

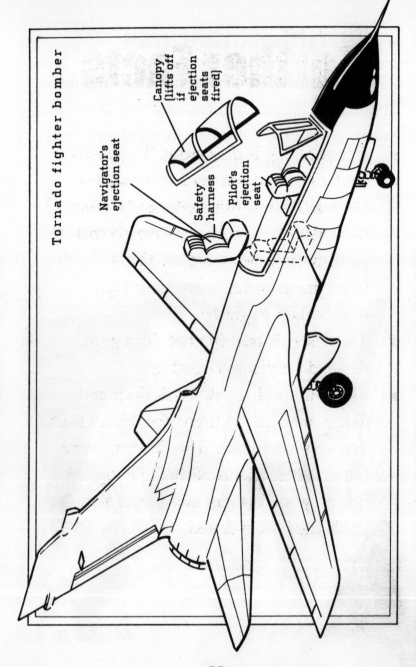

Tornado fighter bomber

Canopy
(lifts off
if
ejection
seats
fired)

Navigator's
ejection seat

Safety
harness

Pilot's
ejection
seat

44

Further Facts

- Desert flying is dangerous. The desert is totally flat and has very few features. Because of this, distances can be hard to work out. The flatness means that pilots have to rely on their flight instruments to tell them how high or low they might be.
- The desert is burning hot during the day and very cold at night.
- The surface of the desert is deep and dangerous and it is only possible to walk at a very slow pace. The Sun was very hot and Peters' and Nichol's flying suits not only made them sweat, but also made them dehydrated.

Glossary

Beacon: a light used to signal position or send a warning in an emergency.

Bedouin: an Arab people who live in the desert.

Camouflage: a disguise that allows the individual to blend in with the surrounding area.

Canopy: in this case, the material of a parachute that spreads out as the parachute opens.

Eject: in this case, to be forcefully thrown out of an aircraft by a special mechanism in the aircraft's seats.

Dehydrated: when someone or something loses liquid.

Formation leader: in this case, the pilot in charge of a group of aircraft.

Friendly airspace: the area of sky over a country that is friendly to the pilots who are flying through it, so the pilots will not be shot at as they cross that country.

Gravity: the force that gives objects weight. Gravity pulls objects towards the Earth.

Haversack: a strong bag that is carried on the back, like a rucksack.

Inflate: to fill with air.

Infra-red: a special type of light that uses radiation to make it visible on certain equipment.

Location: the place where somebody or something is situated.

Military: to do with the armed forces.

Missile: a weapon that can be launched at a target.

Navigator: someone who works out a route.

Resolution: a formal statement made by a committee.

Titanium: a dark-grey, strong, lightweight metal.

Tornado: in this case, a type of fighter aircraft.

Transmitted: when a message or signal is sent.

Turbine: in this instance, the motor of the aircraft.

Vaporized: when a material changes from one state to another. For example, when a liquid changes to a gas, and disappears into the surrounding atmosphere, or air.

Warhead: the section of a missile (usually the tip or head) that contains explosive material.

Important Dates

1991

January 17th
- Tornado jet fighter aircraft attacked by Iraqi SAM-16 missile over desert.

- RAF Flight Lieutenants John Peters and John Nichol eject from aircraft into Iraqi desert.

- Nichol begins transmitting, requesting assistance.

- Peters and Nichol bury as much survival equipment as possible in the sand.

- They begin their desert walk in sweltering conditions.

- The RAF officers see movement in the south.

- They are attacked by an Iraqi patrol and eventually surrender.

March 4th
- After seven weeks' imprisonment Peters and Nichol are released, at the end of the war.